# Libra Horoscope 2025

By
Thalia C. Astraea

# Table of Contents
# <u>Libra (September 23 - October 22)</u>

# Personality

**Libra** (September 23 – October 22), symbolized by the Scales, is an Air sign ruled by Venus, representing balance, harmony, and beauty. Libras are known for their charm, diplomacy, and strong sense of fairness. They thrive in environments that value cooperation and creativity, and they have a natural ability to see all sides of a situation, making them excellent mediators and problem-solvers.

## Core Traits of Libra

1. **Diplomatic and Fair:** Libras are skilled at resolving conflicts and ensuring fairness in any situation. They strive to create harmony in their surroundings.
2. **Charming and Sociable:** With their natural charisma, Libras are excellent conversationalists and are often the center of social gatherings.
3. **Creative and Aesthetic:** Ruled by Venus, Libras have an eye for beauty and often excel in artistic pursuits, design, or fashion.
4. **Balanced and Thoughtful:** They value equilibrium in their personal and professional lives and carefully weigh decisions before acting.

5. **Romantic and Affectionate:** Libras seek meaningful connections and are devoted partners, valuing love and companionship deeply.

## Strengths of Libra

- **Peacemakers:** Their diplomatic nature makes them skilled at mediating conflicts and fostering harmony.
- **Charming:** Libras' friendly and approachable demeanor helps them connect with people easily.
- **Creative Thinkers:** They bring fresh perspectives and innovative ideas to both personal and professional settings.
- **Empathetic:** Libras are attentive listeners and genuinely care about the feelings and perspectives of others.
- **Socially Adept:** They excel in collaborative environments, thriving when working with others toward common goals.

## Weaknesses of Libra

- **Indecisiveness:** Their desire to weigh all options can lead to difficulty in making decisions.
- **People-Pleasing:** Libras may prioritize others' needs over their own, leading to stress or neglect of personal goals.

- **Avoidance of Conflict:** In their pursuit of harmony, they may avoid addressing difficult issues directly.
- **Superficiality:** Their love for beauty and aesthetics may sometimes overshadow deeper priorities.
- **Overdependence:** Libras may seek validation from others, which can affect their self-confidence.

## Libra in Relationships

*As Partners:*

Libras are romantic, devoted, and considerate in relationships. They enjoy creating a loving and harmonious environment for their partner and value emotional connection and intellectual compatibility.

- **Strengths in Love:** Romantic, attentive, and skilled at fostering harmony.
- **Challenges in Love:** Their need for balance may lead to avoiding difficult conversations, and their indecisiveness can frustrate partners.

*As Friends:*

Libras are fun-loving and reliable friends who bring people together and foster positive group dynamics. They are great listeners and often offer wise, balanced advice.

- **Strengths in Friendship:** Sociable, supportive, and inclusive.
- **Challenges in Friendship:** Their tendency to avoid conflict may lead to unspoken tensions in close friendships.

*As Family Members:*

Libras bring warmth and peace to family dynamics. They are often the peacemakers in the household, ensuring everyone feels heard and valued.

## Libra in Career and Professional Life

Libras thrive in careers that involve creativity, collaboration, and diplomacy. They excel in roles that allow them to express their artistic talents or use their interpersonal skills.

*Ideal Career Paths:*

- **Law and Mediation:** Their strong sense of justice makes them excellent lawyers, judges, or mediators.
- **Art and Design:** Careers in fashion, interior design, or the arts align with their aesthetic sensibilities.
- **Public Relations and Marketing:** Their charm and ability to connect with others make them effective in these fields.

- **Counseling and Therapy:** Libras' empathetic nature and desire to help others thrive in counseling roles.
- **Leadership and Team Management:** Their diplomatic approach makes them great leaders who can manage diverse teams effectively.

*Workplace Traits:*

- **Strengths:** Collaborative, creative, and diplomatic, they build strong team relationships and bring innovative ideas to the table.
- **Challenges:** Their indecisiveness may slow down decision-making, and they may avoid addressing workplace conflicts directly.

## Libra and Personal Growth

To unlock their full potential, Libras can benefit from strengthening their decision-making skills and embracing self-confidence.

*Tips for Personal Growth:*

1. **Trust Your Instincts:** Learn to make decisions based on your own needs and values rather than seeking external approval.

2. **Address Conflict Directly:** Confront difficult situations with honesty to foster deeper relationships.
3. **Prioritize Self-Care:** Balance your focus on others' happiness with attention to your own well-being.
4. **Set Clear Goals:** Define your priorities and take steps toward achieving them without overthinking.
5. **Embrace Imperfection:** Accept that not every situation will be perfectly balanced, and focus on progress rather than perfection.

## Libra Compatibility

- **Best Matches:** Gemini, Aquarius, Leo, and Sagittarius—these signs appreciate Libra's charm, creativity, and sociability.
- **Challenging Matches:** Capricorn and Cancer, whose structured and emotional natures may clash with Libra's need for freedom and balance.

## Conclusion

Libras are charismatic, thoughtful, and empathetic individuals who bring beauty and harmony to the world around them. While their pursuit of balance and fairness can sometimes lead to challenges, their creativity, diplomacy, and warmth make them cherished friends, partners, and leaders. By embracing their strengths and addressing their tendencies toward indecision or avoidance, Libras can achieve remarkable success and fulfillment in every aspect of life.

# Introduce

2025 promises to be a transformative and rewarding year for Libra (September 23 – October 22). Symbolized by the Scales and ruled by Venus, Libras are naturally inclined toward balance, harmony, and beauty. This year's celestial alignments will challenge you to embrace change, trust your instincts, and step into new opportunities while maintaining your characteristic diplomacy and grace.

From personal relationships to career achievements, 2025 encourages you to strike a balance between your external responsibilities and inner growth. Here's an in-depth look at what this year holds for Libras.

**Overall Energy for Libra in 2025**

The year begins with Jupiter in Taurus, emphasizing themes of financial stability, transformation, and emotional depth. This placement encourages Libras to build a secure foundation in their personal and professional lives while exploring their emotional needs. Saturn's presence in Pisces continues to highlight self-discipline and responsibility, urging you to take a pragmatic approach to your goals.

As Jupiter transitions into Gemini mid-year, the energy shifts toward intellectual pursuits, communication, and expanding your social horizons. The latter half of the year inspires creativity, travel, and learning, allowing Libras to broaden their perspectives and forge meaningful connections.

Pluto's transit into Aquarius brings a transformative influence in matters of self-expression and personal identity. You'll find yourself exploring new ways to align with your authentic self, unlocking fresh opportunities for personal growth and fulfillment.

**Career and Ambition**

2025 is a year of career advancement and professional growth for Libra. Jupiter's influence in Taurus during the first half of the year emphasizes stability and long-term planning, making it an excellent time to refine your strategies and focus on your goals.

- **Key Opportunities:** Networking, creative projects, and leadership roles are favored this year. Collaborative efforts will open doors, and your natural charm and diplomacy will be instrumental in achieving success.

- **Challenges:** Balancing your need for harmony with the demands of your career may feel challenging, especially during busy periods. Trust your instincts and avoid overcommitting.

**Tips for Career Success in 2025:**

1. Prioritize organization and clear communication in all professional endeavors.
2. Embrace change and adaptability, especially as new opportunities arise mid-year.
3. Focus on building relationships with colleagues and mentors to expand your professional network.

**Finance and Wealth**

Financial stability and growth are central themes for Libra in 2025. Jupiter's presence in Taurus supports disciplined saving and wise investments, while Saturn in Pisces encourages cautious decision-making.

- **Key Opportunities:** The first half of the year is ideal for revisiting your budget, exploring new income streams, and consolidating financial stability. Unexpected financial gains or rewards for past efforts may also arise.
- **Challenges:** Avoid impulsive spending, especially during moments of celebration or stress.

## Tips for Financial Success in 2025:

1. Create a realistic financial plan and stick to it.
2. Focus on building an emergency fund to prepare for unexpected expenses.
3. Seek advice if considering major investments or financial decisions.

## Love and Relationships

In 2025, relationships take center stage for Libra. Venus, your ruling planet, ensures that love, connection, and harmony are recurring themes throughout the year. Whether single or in a relationship, you'll find opportunities to deepen emotional bonds and experience meaningful growth in your personal connections.

- **For Singles:** The first half of the year may bring romantic opportunities through work, travel, or social events. Look for partners who resonate with your values and long-term vision. Relationships formed this year have the potential for emotional depth and stability.
- **For Those in Relationships:** This is a year to strengthen trust and intimacy. Open communication, shared experiences, and thoughtful gestures will nurture your bond and help you navigate any challenges.

**Challenges in Love:**

- The need for balance may cause you to avoid difficult conversations. Trust that addressing issues directly will strengthen your relationships.
- Maintaining independence within your partnerships may feel challenging at times.

**Tips for Love and Relationships in 2025:**

1. Practice active listening and empathy to build deeper connections.
2. Be open to vulnerability and honest communication.
3. Celebrate milestones and cherish shared experiences with your partner.

**Health and Wellness**

Health is an area of focus for Libra in 2025, with Saturn in Pisces urging you to establish sustainable routines that support your overall well-being.

- **Physical Health:** The disciplined energy of Saturn will inspire you to adopt healthier habits, such as regular exercise, mindful eating, and prioritizing rest. Activities like yoga, swimming, or walking will help you maintain balance and flexibility.

- **Mental and Emotional Health:** Jupiter's influence in Taurus encourages you to prioritize self-care and emotional resilience. Reflective practices like journaling or meditation will help you stay grounded.

## Challenges in Health:

Balancing your busy schedule with self-care may feel challenging at times. Remember to set aside moments for relaxation and rejuvenation.

## Tips for Health and Wellness in 2025:

1. Incorporate mindfulness techniques into your daily routine to reduce stress.
2. Prioritize consistency in fitness and nutrition without striving for perfection.
3. Focus on creating a balanced work-life schedule to avoid burnout.

## Personal Growth and Spirituality

2025 is a transformative year for Libra, with Pluto's influence in Aquarius encouraging you to explore your authentic self and embrace new ways of expressing your creativity.

- **Key Themes:** Self-discovery, emotional growth, and creative expression will define your journey this year.
- **Opportunities for Growth:** Explore artistic or intellectual pursuits that inspire you. Engage in activities that align with your personal values and bring you joy.

## Tips for Personal Growth in 2025:

1. Trust your instincts and let go of the need for external validation.
2. Embrace new experiences and step out of your comfort zone.
3. Focus on progress, not perfection, as you work toward personal and professional goals.

## Key Dates for Libra in 2025

- **February 14:** A Full Moon in Leo highlights creativity and encourages bold self-expression.
- **April 8:** A New Moon in Aries inspires fresh starts in relationships and partnerships.
- **October 23 – November 21:** The Sun in Scorpio deepens your focus on transformation and emotional growth.

## Challenges for Libra in 2025

- Balancing your natural desire for harmony with the need to assert your boundaries.
- Overthinking or delaying decisions due to a desire to weigh all options.
- Managing stress from juggling personal and professional responsibilities.

## Conclusion

2025 is a year of balance, growth, and transformation for Libra. By embracing new opportunities, nurturing meaningful relationships, and focusing on personal well-being, you'll create harmony and success in every area of your life. Trust your instincts, stay adaptable, and celebrate the beauty of progress and connection as you navigate this exciting year.

Libra, the universe is aligned to support your growth and fulfillment in 2025—step forward with grace and confidence!

# January

January 2025 sets the stage for a year of growth and balance for Libra. With the Sun in Capricorn for most of the month, the focus is on structure, long-term planning, and building a solid foundation for success. This energy is ideal for organizing your professional life, reassessing your finances, and fostering meaningful relationships.

## ***Work***

January encourages discipline and strategic planning in your professional life.

- **Opportunities:** The Capricorn energy supports setting long-term goals, refining work processes, and building professional relationships. Mid-month, you may gain recognition for past efforts or be presented with new opportunities.
- **Challenges:** Balancing your need for harmony with the demands of a structured environment may feel challenging. Avoid procrastination or indecisiveness.

**Advice:** Use the structured Capricorn energy to prioritize your goals and take consistent, focused steps toward success.

<u>*Finance*</u>

Your financial outlook in January highlights thoughtful planning and cautious spending.

- **Opportunities:** This is a good time to revisit your budget, set savings goals, and plan for major expenses later in the year. Financial rewards may come from efforts made in the past year.
- **Challenges:** Avoid impulsive spending, particularly on luxuries or social events.

**Advice:** Focus on creating a solid financial plan that aligns with your long-term goals. Prioritize saving over unnecessary purchases.

<u>*Love*</u>

January brings warmth and reflection to Libra's love life.

- **For Singles:** You may meet someone through work, family connections, or social gatherings. Take your time to build trust and compatibility.
- **For Those in Relationships:** Focus on strengthening the bond with your partner by addressing any unresolved issues with patience and understanding. Shared activities and open communication will deepen your connection.

**Advice:** Be authentic and open about your feelings. Use the Capricorn energy to nurture stability and commitment in your relationships.

## *Health*

Health-wise, January encourages Libra to focus on creating balance and consistency in wellness routines.

- **Strengths:** The Capricorn energy inspires discipline, making it an excellent time to adopt or refine healthy habits. Activities like yoga, stretching, or walking will help you maintain physical and mental well-being.
- **Challenges:** Stress from work or personal responsibilities may impact your energy levels if not managed effectively.

**Advice:** Incorporate mindfulness practices into your daily routine to reduce stress. Ensure you're getting enough rest, staying hydrated, and eating balanced meals.

## *Be Careful*

- **Overanalyzing:** Avoid spending too much time weighing options, especially in work or financial matters. Trust your instincts.

- **Neglecting Self-Care:** Don't let work or personal obligations interfere with your need for rest and relaxation.
- **Procrastination:** Stay focused and proactive, even when decisions feel challenging.

## *Advice*

1. **Organize and Prioritize:** Use the disciplined Capricorn energy to set clear goals and develop actionable plans.
2. **Focus on Relationships:** Strengthen connections by being present and expressing appreciation for loved ones.
3. **Practice Self-Care:** Balance your ambitions with relaxation and mindfulness to maintain energy and clarity.

## *Additional Tips*

- **Lucky Days:** January 10, 18, and 28 – Ideal for making decisions, creative projects, or fostering relationships.
- **Lucky Color:** Navy Blue – This color symbolizes focus, stability, and clarity.
- **Affirmation for January:** *"I align my actions with my values, creating harmony and success in all areas of my life."*

January 2025 is a month of grounding and preparation for Libra. By focusing on thoughtful planning, meaningful connections, and self-care, you'll set the stage for a fulfilling and balanced year ahead.

# February

February 2025 is a month of creativity, connection, and thoughtful progress for Libra. With the Sun in Aquarius for most of the month, your focus will be on intellectual pursuits, social connections, and exploring innovative ideas. As the Sun transitions into Pisces later in February, the energy becomes more introspective and emotional, encouraging you to nurture your inner self and build meaningful relationships.

## *Work*

February emphasizes collaboration and creativity in Libra's professional life.

- **Opportunities:** The Aquarius energy supports brainstorming, teamwork, and pursuing innovative projects. Mid-month is an excellent time to network, present ideas, or seek partnerships. The Pisces energy later in the month encourages thoughtful reflection and refining your strategies.
- **Challenges:** Balancing your creative energy with the need for structure may feel challenging. Avoid overcommitting to too many tasks.

**Advice:** Use Aquarius energy to think outside the box and the Pisces influence to align your goals with your deeper values.

## *Finance*

Your financial outlook in February encourages mindful spending and cautious planning.

- **Opportunities:** Financial gains may come from collaborative efforts, creative ventures, or networking opportunities. This is a good time to reassess your budget and set savings goals.
- **Challenges:** Avoid impulsive purchases, particularly on social or lifestyle-related expenses.

**Advice:** Stick to your financial plan and focus on building long-term stability. Prioritize saving for future goals over short-term indulgences.

## *Love*

February brings warmth and connection to Libra's love life, with Venus enhancing harmony and romance.

- **For Singles:** Social events, creative activities, or networking opportunities may lead to promising romantic connections. Look for someone who shares your intellectual and emotional values.

- **For Those in Relationships:** Focus on nurturing emotional intimacy and resolving any lingering issues with your partner. Shared activities and open communication will strengthen your bond.

**Advice:** Be open and genuine in your interactions. Use the Pisces energy later in the month to deepen emotional connections and celebrate love in all its forms.

## *Health*

Health-wise, February encourages Libra to maintain balance and focus on emotional and physical well-being.

- **Strengths:** The Aquarius energy supports staying active and engaging in group activities or hobbies that boost mental and physical health.
- **Challenges:** Increased social or work commitments may lead to stress if not managed effectively.

**Advice:** Incorporate mindfulness practices into your routine to stay grounded. Focus on maintaining a balanced diet, staying hydrated, and getting enough rest to recharge.

## *Be Careful*

- **Overcommitting:** Avoid taking on too many responsibilities, as this could lead to stress or burnout.
- **Emotional Decisions:** Think carefully before making impulsive choices, particularly in finances or relationships.
- **Neglecting Balance:** Don't let external demands overshadow your need for relaxation and self-care.

## *Advice*

1. **Collaborate and Connect:** Use the dynamic Aquarius energy to foster teamwork and build meaningful connections.
2. **Reflect and Refine:** Embrace the Pisces influence later in the month to reassess your priorities and nurture emotional well-being.
3. **Prioritize Balance:** Maintain harmony by balancing productivity with moments of rest and introspection.

## *Additional Tips*

- **Lucky Days:** February 8, 14, and 27 – Perfect for networking, creative pursuits, or deepening relationships.
- **Lucky Color:** Sky Blue – This color symbolizes clarity, calm, and intellectual growth.

- **Affirmation for February:** *"I balance connection and reflection, creating harmony and success in my life."*

February 2025 is a month of inspiration and connection for Libra. By focusing on collaboration, thoughtful planning, and self-care, you'll navigate this dynamic period with confidence and clarity.

# March

March 2025 is a month of introspection, connection, and forward momentum for Libra. With the Sun in Pisces for most of the month, the focus will be on emotional well-being, creativity, and nurturing your relationships. As the Sun transitions into Aries later in March, the energy shifts to action, ambition, and partnerships, making this a dynamic time to balance reflection with decisive steps forward.

## *Work*

March emphasizes creativity and collaboration in Libra's professional life.

- **Opportunities:** The Pisces energy supports creative problem-solving, refining ongoing projects, and building strong professional relationships. The Aries influence later in the month inspires boldness and a proactive approach to achieving your goals.
- **Challenges:** Emotional distractions or overthinking may slow your progress early in the month. Avoid procrastination and trust your instincts.

**Advice:** Use the reflective Pisces energy to fine-tune your strategies and the confident Aries energy to take action on well-thought-out plans.

## *Finance*

Your financial outlook in March highlights discipline and cautious spending.

- **Opportunities:** Creative or collaborative ventures may yield moderate financial rewards. This is a good time to reassess your financial goals and focus on building a stable foundation.
- **Challenges:** Avoid impulsive spending, especially as the Aries energy later in the month may tempt you to indulge in spontaneous purchases.

**Advice:** Stick to your budget and prioritize long-term financial security. Consider consulting a financial advisor if planning significant investments or changes.

## *Love*

March brings warmth and growth to Libra's love life, with Venus fostering connection and emotional depth.

- **For Singles:** You may meet someone through creative activities, social gatherings, or shared interests. Emotional compatibility will play a significant role in new connections.

- **For Those in Relationships:** Focus on deepening emotional intimacy and resolving any lingering misunderstandings. The Aries energy later in the month inspires passion and shared adventures.

**Advice:** Be open and genuine in your interactions. Use the Pisces energy to nurture emotional bonds and the Aries energy to reignite excitement and spontaneity.

## *Health*

Health-wise, March encourages Libra to focus on balance and emotional well-being.

- **Strengths:** The Pisces energy inspires self-care practices such as yoga, meditation, or creative hobbies that promote mental and physical health.
- **Challenges:** Stress from juggling responsibilities may impact your energy levels if not managed properly.

**Advice:** Incorporate mindfulness practices into your routine to stay grounded. Maintain a balanced diet, stay hydrated, and get plenty of rest to recharge.

## *Be Careful*

- **Overthinking:** Avoid letting your analytical mind dwell on past mistakes or future uncertainties. Focus on the present.

- **Impulsiveness:** Think carefully before making major financial or personal commitments.
- **Neglecting Balance:** Ensure you're prioritizing self-care alongside your professional and personal responsibilities.

## *Advice*

1. **Reflect and Refine:** Use the introspective Pisces energy to align your goals with your values and prepare for bold action.
2. **Take Action with Confidence:** Embrace the dynamic Aries energy to make decisive moves in your career and personal life.
3. **Nurture Relationships:** Invest time in meaningful connections and express appreciation for the people who support you.

## *Additional Tips*

- **Lucky Days:** March 7, 14, and 26 – Ideal for decision-making, creative pursuits, or deepening relationships.
- **Lucky Color:** Lavender – This color symbolizes calm, creativity, and emotional balance.
- **Affirmation for March:** *"I balance reflection with action, creating harmony and success in my life."*

March 2025 is a month of growth and connection for Libra. By focusing on thoughtful planning, meaningful relationships, and balanced self-care, you'll navigate this transformative period with confidence and clarity.

# April

April 2025 is a month of dynamism, connection, and strategic planning for Libra. With the Sun in Aries for most of the month, the focus will be on partnerships, taking action, and achieving balance between personal and professional responsibilities. As the Sun transitions into Taurus later in April, the energy shifts to stability, financial growth, and nurturing your sense of security. This blend of boldness and practicality makes April a powerful month for personal and career development.

## *Work*

April emphasizes collaboration and proactive decision-making in Libra's professional life.

- **Opportunities:** The Aries energy supports taking bold steps in your career, such as pitching ideas, pursuing leadership roles, or starting new projects. The Taurus influence later in the month helps you stabilize and refine these initiatives for long-term success.
- **Challenges:** Balancing your natural inclination toward harmony with the fast-paced Aries energy may feel overwhelming. Avoid procrastination or overthinking.

**Advice:** Use Aries' momentum to take decisive action and Taurus' grounding energy to create practical plans and follow through on commitments.

## *Finance*

Your financial outlook in April highlights growth and careful planning.

- **Opportunities:** This is a good time to explore new income opportunities, reassess your budget, and focus on saving for future goals. Financial gains may come from creative efforts or partnerships.
- **Challenges:** Avoid impulsive spending, particularly during Aries season when you may feel driven by momentary excitement.

**Advice:** Stick to a financial plan that prioritizes long-term stability. Use Taurus' practical energy later in the month to make thoughtful financial decisions.

## *Love*

April brings excitement and warmth to Libra's love life, with Venus fostering connection and passion.

- **For Singles:** New romantic opportunities may arise through social events, work, or mutual friends. The Aries energy inspires confidence, making it a great time to explore new connections.

- **For Those in Relationships:** Focus on balancing passion and emotional intimacy with your partner. Late April is ideal for planning meaningful moments together to strengthen your bond.

**Advice:** Be authentic and open about your feelings. Use the Taurus energy to nurture stability and commitment in your relationships.

## *Health*

Health-wise, April encourages Libra to balance activity and rest to maintain well-being.

- **Strengths:** The Aries energy inspires physical activity, making it a great time to enhance your fitness routine or try new exercises.
- **Challenges:** Overexertion or neglecting self-care may lead to fatigue if not managed properly.

**Advice:** Incorporate relaxation techniques like yoga or meditation into your daily routine. Focus on staying hydrated, eating balanced meals, and ensuring adequate sleep to recharge.

## *Be Careful*

- **Impulsiveness:** Avoid making hasty decisions in work or financial matters without thoroughly considering your options.

- **Overcommitment:** Don't take on too many responsibilities, as this could lead to stress or burnout.
- **Neglecting Balance:** Ensure you're devoting time to both personal relationships and professional goals.

## *Advice*

1. **Take Decisive Steps:** Use Aries' dynamic energy to take bold actions and make progress toward your goals.
2. **Focus on Stability:** As Taurus season begins, shift your attention to building a secure foundation for the future.
3. **Nurture Relationships:** Strengthen connections through thoughtful communication and shared experiences.

## *Additional Tips*

- **Lucky Days:** April 9, 18, and 28 – Perfect for decision-making, pursuing creative projects, or fostering relationships.
- **Lucky Color:** Emerald Green – This color symbolizes growth, balance, and stability.
- **Affirmation for April:** *"I balance bold action with thoughtful planning, creating harmony and success in my life."*

April 2025 is a month of excitement and grounding for Libra. By focusing on meaningful connections, thoughtful planning, and self-care, you'll navigate this dynamic period with confidence and clarity.

# May

May 2025 is a month of stability, introspection, and growth for Libra. With the Sun in Taurus for most of the month, the focus will be on grounding yourself, creating financial security, and nurturing relationships. As the Sun transitions into Gemini later in May, the energy shifts to communication, curiosity, and expanding your social and intellectual horizons. This blend of steady progress and dynamic interaction makes May a productive and fulfilling month.

## *Work*

May emphasizes organization and steady progress in Libra's professional life.

- **Opportunities:** The Taurus energy supports careful planning and long-term strategies. Mid-month is ideal for revisiting ongoing projects, refining processes, and building on your achievements. The Gemini energy later in the month inspires fresh ideas and dynamic discussions with colleagues.
- **Challenges:** Avoid becoming too rigid in your approach or overanalyzing minor details, as this could slow progress.

**Advice:** Use the grounded Taurus energy to focus on key priorities and the flexible Gemini energy to explore creative solutions and collaborations.

## *Finance*

Your financial outlook in May highlights discipline and potential growth.

- **Opportunities:** Financial stability improves through careful budgeting, disciplined saving, or investments made earlier in the year. This is also a favorable time to plan for future expenses or reassess your financial goals.
- **Challenges:** Avoid impulsive spending, especially as Gemini's social energy may tempt you to indulge in spontaneous activities.

**Advice:** Stick to your financial plan and prioritize long-term security over short-term gratification.

## *Love*

May brings warmth and harmony to Libra's love life, with Venus fostering connection and emotional intimacy.

- **For Singles:** This is a great time to meet someone through shared interests, work, or social gatherings. Emotional compatibility will play a significant role in new connections.

- **For Those in Relationships:** Focus on strengthening trust and emotional closeness with your partner. Shared experiences and honest communication will deepen your bond.

**Advice:** Use the Taurus energy to nurture emotional stability and the Gemini energy to keep things lighthearted and fun.

## *Health*

Health-wise, May encourages Libra to maintain balance and consistency in their wellness routines.

- **Strengths:** The Taurus energy supports grounding practices like yoga, mindful eating, or outdoor activities that enhance both mental and physical well-being.
- **Challenges:** Stress from juggling responsibilities may impact your energy levels if not managed effectively.

**Advice:** Incorporate relaxation techniques into your daily routine. Stay consistent with exercise and focus on nourishing your body with healthy, balanced meals.

## Be Careful

- **Overindulgence:** Avoid overcommitting to social activities or indulging in unhealthy habits.
- **Neglecting Details:** While focusing on the bigger picture, don't overlook important details in work or financial matters.
- **Rushed Decisions:** Take your time with major commitments to ensure they align with your long-term goals.

## Advice

1. **Ground Yourself:** Use Taurus energy to focus on stability, security, and building a solid foundation for the future.
2. **Embrace Curiosity:** As Gemini season begins, explore new ideas, engage in conversations, and expand your horizons.
3. **Nurture Relationships:** Strengthen emotional connections by being present and open with your loved ones.

## Additional Tips

- **Lucky Days:** May 8, 16, and 27 – Ideal for decision-making, creative projects, or strengthening relationships.

- **Lucky Color:** Earthy Brown – This color symbolizes grounding, stability, and resilience.
- **Affirmation for May:** *"I create stability and connection, aligning my actions with my values and dreams."*

May 2025 is a month of steady progress and connection for Libra. By focusing on thoughtful planning, meaningful relationships, and balanced self-care, you'll navigate this productive period with clarity and confidence.

# June

June 2025 is a month of exploration, communication, and personal growth for Libra. With the Sun in Gemini for most of the month, the focus is on expanding your horizons, building relationships, and pursuing intellectual and creative interests. As the Sun transitions into Cancer later in June, the energy shifts toward introspection, emotional depth, and creating a sense of security in your personal and professional life.

### *Work*

June emphasizes networking and adaptability in Libra's professional life.

- **Opportunities:** The Gemini energy supports brainstorming, collaboration, and exploring innovative solutions. This is an excellent time to engage in discussions, present ideas, or attend events that expand your professional network. The Cancer influence later in the month encourages you to focus on long-term strategies and build strong, supportive relationships at work.
- **Challenges:** Balancing your natural preference for harmony with Gemini's fast-paced energy may feel challenging. Avoid overextending yourself.

**Advice:** Use early June to embrace dynamic opportunities and the reflective Cancer energy to realign your career goals with your personal values.

## *Finance*

Your financial outlook in June encourages thoughtful decision-making and cautious planning.

- **Opportunities:** Creative projects or side ventures may bring additional income. This is also a good time to revisit your budget and evaluate future financial goals.
- **Challenges:** Avoid impulsive spending, particularly on travel, social events, or luxury items.

**Advice:** Focus on saving and stick to your financial plan. Consider consulting a professional if exploring major investments or new income opportunities.

## *Love*

June brings warmth and excitement to Libra's love life, with Venus enhancing connection and communication.

- **For Singles:** Social gatherings, intellectual pursuits, or travel opportunities may lead to exciting romantic connections. Look for someone who shares your curiosity and zest for life.
- **For Those in Relationships:** Focus on nurturing open communication and shared experiences with your partner. The Cancer energy later in the month encourages emotional closeness and intimacy.

**Advice:** Be authentic and attentive in your interactions. Use the dynamic Gemini energy to keep things lively and the nurturing Cancer energy to deepen emotional bonds.

## *Health*

Health-wise, June encourages Libra to maintain balance and prioritize wellness amidst a busy schedule.

- **Strengths:** The Gemini energy inspires physical activity and mental stimulation, making it a great time for outdoor exercises, group activities, or hobbies that keep you engaged.
- **Challenges:** Stress from juggling responsibilities may affect your energy levels if not managed effectively.

**Advice:** Incorporate relaxation techniques such as yoga, meditation, or journaling into your routine. Focus on maintaining a balanced diet, staying hydrated, and ensuring you're getting enough rest to recharge.

## *Be Careful*

- **Overcommitting:** Avoid taking on too many social or professional obligations, as this could lead to stress or burnout.
- **Impulsiveness:** Think carefully before making significant financial or personal decisions.
- **Neglecting Emotional Needs:** Balance your active schedule with time for self-reflection and nurturing emotional well-being.

## *Advice*

1. **Explore and Communicate:** Use Gemini's dynamic energy to expand your horizons, engage in meaningful conversations, and build connections.

2. **Focus on Emotional Depth:** Embrace the Cancer influence later in the month to strengthen relationships and align your goals with your inner values.
3. **Prioritize Balance:** Maintain harmony by balancing productivity with rest and relaxation.

## *Additional Tips*

- **Lucky Days:** June 7, 15, and 26 – Perfect for networking, decision-making, or creative pursuits.
- **Lucky Color:** Light Yellow – This color symbolizes positivity, clarity, and intellectual growth.
- **Affirmation for June:** *"I balance exploration and reflection, creating harmony and growth in my life."*

June 2025 is a month of dynamic opportunities and introspection for Libra. By focusing on meaningful connections, thoughtful planning, and balanced self-care, you'll navigate this vibrant period with confidence and clarity.

# July

July 2025 is a month of introspection, connection, and steady progress for Libra. With the Sun in Cancer for most of the month, the focus is on nurturing relationships, emotional well-being, and building a sense of security in your personal and professional life. As the Sun transitions into Leo later in the month, the energy becomes more dynamic, encouraging self-expression, creativity, and social engagement.

## *Work*

July emphasizes reflection and preparation in Libra's professional life.

- **Opportunities:** The Cancer energy supports strengthening relationships with colleagues and reassessing long-term career goals. Late in the month, the Leo influence inspires boldness and creativity, making it an excellent time to pitch innovative ideas or take on leadership roles.
- **Challenges:** Emotional distractions or overthinking may slow down progress early in the month. Avoid letting perfectionism hinder your ability to act.

**Advice:** Use the introspective Cancer energy to refine your plans and the confident Leo energy to take decisive action. Stay balanced and adaptable to navigate challenges effectively.

## _Finance_

Your financial outlook in July emphasizes stability and careful planning.

- **Opportunities:** Small financial gains may come from past efforts or disciplined savings. This is a favorable time to focus on budget adjustments and plan for upcoming expenses.
- **Challenges:** Avoid emotional spending, especially during moments of stress or celebration.

**Advice:** Stick to your financial goals and prioritize long-term stability over short-term gratification. Reassess your financial strategies to ensure they align with your priorities.

## _Love_

July brings warmth and depth to Libra's love life, with Venus fostering emotional connection and intimacy.

- **For Singles:** This is an excellent time to meet someone new through shared interests, family connections, or social gatherings. Look for a relationship that resonates with your values and emotional needs.

- **For Those in Relationships:** Focus on nurturing emotional intimacy and creating meaningful moments with your partner. The Leo energy later in the month encourages playful and adventurous bonding.

**Advice:** Be authentic and open in your interactions. Use the Cancer energy to deepen emotional bonds and the Leo energy to keep your relationships lively and exciting.

## *Health*

Health-wise, July encourages Libra to maintain emotional and physical balance.

- **Strengths:** The Cancer energy supports self-care practices like journaling, meditation, or spending time with loved ones.
- **Challenges:** Stress from personal or professional responsibilities may affect your energy levels if not managed effectively.

**Advice:** Focus on relaxation and maintaining consistency in wellness routines. Ensure you're staying hydrated, eating balanced meals, and getting enough rest to recharge.

## *Be Careful*

- **Overthinking:** Avoid dwelling on past mistakes or uncertainties, as this could lead to unnecessary stress.
- **Emotional Decisions:** Think carefully before making major financial or personal commitments during emotional moments.
- **Neglecting Self-Care:** Balance your active schedule with adequate downtime to maintain well-being.

## *Advice*

1. **Reflect and Reassess:** Use the Cancer energy to align your actions with your values and nurture emotional stability.
2. **Take Bold Steps:** Embrace the Leo energy later in the month to pursue creative and social opportunities with confidence.
3. **Prioritize Relationships:** Invest time in meaningful connections and show appreciation for loved ones.

## *Additional Tips*

- **Lucky Days:** July 9, 17, and 27 – Ideal for decision-making, creative projects, or nurturing relationships.
- **Lucky Color:** Pale Pink – This color symbolizes harmony, compassion, and emotional clarity.

- **Affirmation for July:** *"I align my actions with my values, creating harmony and success in all areas of my life."*

July 2025 is a month of growth and connection for Libra. By focusing on meaningful relationships, thoughtful planning, and balanced self-care, you'll navigate this dynamic period with clarity and confidence.

# August

August 2025 is a vibrant and empowering month for Libra, filled with opportunities for self-expression, social engagement, and personal growth. With the Sun in Leo for most of the month, the focus is on creativity, leadership, and strengthening your social connections. As the Sun transitions into Virgo later in August, the energy shifts toward introspection, organization, and laying the groundwork for future success. This blend of boldness and practicality makes August a month of dynamic opportunities and thoughtful preparation.

## *Work*

August emphasizes leadership and creativity in Libra's professional life.

- **Opportunities:** The Leo energy supports taking bold initiatives, presenting innovative ideas, and stepping into leadership roles. Late in the month, the Virgo influence helps you refine your plans and focus on the details needed to achieve long-term goals.
- **Challenges:** Balancing your natural desire for harmony with the assertive energy of Leo may feel challenging. Avoid procrastination or overanalyzing decisions.

**Advice:** Use the Leo energy to embrace bold action and the Virgo energy to ensure your plans are realistic and well-organized.

## *Finance*

Your financial outlook in August highlights careful planning and potential rewards.

- **Opportunities:** Financial gains may come from creative projects, side ventures, or efforts you've been nurturing over the past months. This is also a good time to review your budget and align your spending with your priorities.
- **Challenges:** Avoid overspending on luxuries or social activities during the high-energy Leo season.

**Advice:** Stick to a disciplined financial plan and prioritize saving for future investments or goals.

## *Love*

August brings passion and excitement to Libra's love life, with Venus enhancing connection and romance.

- **For Singles:** You'll attract attention with your charisma and charm, making it a great time to meet someone new. Social gatherings, creative pursuits, or community events may lead to meaningful romantic connections.

- **For Those in Relationships:** Focus on keeping the spark alive with thoughtful gestures, shared adventures, and open communication. Late August is ideal for discussing long-term plans and deepening your bond.

**Advice:** Be authentic and confident in your interactions. Use the Leo energy to celebrate love and the Virgo energy to nurture emotional stability in your relationships.

## *Health*

Health-wise, August encourages Libra to maintain consistency and focus on overall well-being.

- **Strengths:** The Leo energy inspires physical activity and confidence, making it a great time to start or enhance a fitness routine.
- **Challenges:** Overexertion or neglecting rest during the busy Leo season may lead to fatigue if not managed properly.

**Advice:** Incorporate relaxation techniques like yoga or meditation into your routine. Focus on maintaining a balanced diet, staying hydrated, and ensuring you get enough rest to recharge.

## *Be Careful*

- **Overindulgence:** Avoid overspending or overcommitting during moments of excitement or celebration.
- **Impulsiveness:** Think carefully before making major decisions in financial or personal matters.
- **Neglecting Details:** While focusing on the big picture, don't overlook important details, especially as Virgo season begins.

## _Advice_

1. **Step into the Spotlight:** Use the bold Leo energy to take initiative and express your creativity with confidence.
2. **Plan with Precision:** As Virgo season begins, focus on organizing your goals and refining your strategies for success.
3. **Nurture Relationships:** Invest time in building meaningful connections and showing appreciation for loved ones.

## _Additional Tips_

- **Lucky Days:** August 11, 19, and 29 – Perfect for decision-making, creative pursuits, or fostering relationships.
- **Lucky Color:** Gold – This color symbolizes confidence, success, and positivity.

- **Affirmation for August:** *"I embrace my creativity and align my actions with my purpose, creating harmony and success in all areas of my life."*

August 2025 is a month of bold action and thoughtful preparation for Libra. By balancing creativity with discipline and focusing on meaningful connections, you'll make the most of this dynamic and fulfilling period.

# September

September 2025 is a month of reflection, preparation, and empowerment for Libra. With the Sun in Virgo for most of the month, the focus is on organization, introspection, and setting the stage for personal and professional success. As the Sun transitions into your sign later in September, you'll feel a surge of confidence, charm, and energy, making this a time to step into the spotlight and embrace new opportunities.

## *Work*

September emphasizes productivity and long-term planning in Libra's professional life.

- **Opportunities:** The Virgo energy supports refining your strategies, addressing details, and creating a solid foundation for future success. As the Sun moves into Libra, your natural charisma and diplomacy will help you gain support for your ideas and projects.
- **Challenges:** Overanalyzing or striving for perfection may slow down progress early in the month. Avoid getting stuck in minor details.

**Advice:** Use Virgo season to organize and strategize, and embrace Libra season to take decisive action and shine in your professional endeavors.

## *Finance*

Your financial outlook in September highlights stability and thoughtful planning.

- **Opportunities:** This is a favorable time to reassess your budget, prioritize savings, and make steady progress toward your financial goals. Small but meaningful gains may come from past efforts or disciplined spending.
- **Challenges:** Avoid impulsive financial decisions, especially as you transition into Libra season's social and celebratory energy.

**Advice:** Stick to your budget and focus on building financial security. Align your spending with your long-term goals.

## *Love*

September brings warmth and harmony to Libra's love life, with Venus fostering emotional connection and balance.

- **For Singles:** You'll feel a renewed sense of confidence and charm, making it a great time to meet someone new. Look for romantic opportunities through work, social events, or mutual friends.

- **For Those in Relationships:** Focus on strengthening your bond with your partner by addressing unresolved issues and planning meaningful moments together. The Libra energy later in the month inspires romance and excitement.

**Advice:** Be authentic and open about your feelings. Use Virgo energy to nurture emotional stability and Libra energy to celebrate love and connection.

## *Health*

Health-wise, September encourages Libra to focus on creating balance and consistency in their wellness routines.

- **Strengths:** The Virgo energy supports mindful practices like yoga, meditation, or healthy eating habits that enhance both mental and physical well-being.
- **Challenges:** Stress from balancing work and personal responsibilities may affect your energy levels if not managed effectively.

**Advice:** Prioritize rest and relaxation. Maintain consistency in exercise and nutrition, and incorporate activities that bring you joy and calm.

### _Be Careful_

- **Overanalyzing:** Avoid getting stuck in perfectionist tendencies, as this can lead to unnecessary stress.
- **Neglecting Relationships:** Don't let your focus on work overshadow your personal connections.
- **Impulsiveness:** Think carefully before making major financial or personal commitments.

### _Advice_

1. **Refine and Realign:** Use Virgo season to organize your plans and ensure they align with your goals and values.
2. **Celebrate Yourself:** Embrace Libra season's energy to step into the spotlight, build connections, and pursue opportunities.

**Maintain Balance:** Focus on self-care and meaningful relationships to sustain energy and harmony.

<u>*Additional Tips*</u>

- **Lucky Days:** September 7, 15, and 24 – Ideal for decision-making, creative pursuits, or strengthening relationships.
- **Lucky Color:** Ivory White – This color symbolizes clarity, balance, and renewal.
- **Affirmation for September:** *"I align my plans with my purpose, creating harmony and success in all areas of my life."*

September 2025 is a month of preparation and empowerment for Libra. By balancing introspection with action and focusing on meaningful connections, you'll navigate this transformative period with confidence and clarity.

# October

October 2025 is a dynamic and empowering month for Libra as the Sun illuminates your sign for most of the month. This is a time for celebration, self-expression, and new beginnings. With your natural charm and diplomacy enhanced, you'll find opportunities to shine in personal relationships, professional endeavors, and social circles. As the Sun transitions into Scorpio later in October, the energy deepens, encouraging introspection, emotional growth, and strategic planning.

## *Work*

October emphasizes creativity and leadership in Libra's professional life.

- **Opportunities:** The Libra energy supports showcasing your talents, leading projects, and collaborating with others. Mid-month is ideal for pitching ideas, networking, or pursuing new career opportunities. The Scorpio energy later in the month inspires focus and long-term strategic thinking.
- **Challenges:** Balancing your natural desire for harmony with the need to assert yourself may feel

challenging. Avoid hesitation when presenting your ideas or pursuing leadership roles.

**Advice:** Use Libra energy to connect and inspire and Scorpio energy to dive into complex tasks and refine your goals.

## *Finance*

Your financial outlook in October highlights balance and potential growth.

- **Opportunities:** Financial rewards may come from creative or collaborative efforts. This is a favorable time to reassess your budget and explore new ways to grow your savings or investments.
- **Challenges:** Avoid impulsive spending, especially on social events or luxuries, as Libra season's celebratory energy may tempt indulgence.

**Advice:** Focus on aligning your financial decisions with your long-term goals. Prioritize saving and disciplined planning over short-term gratification.

## *Love*

October is a romantic and emotionally fulfilling month for Libra, with Venus enhancing harmony and connection.

- **For Singles:** You'll attract attention effortlessly, making it an excellent time to meet new people. Romantic opportunities may arise through social gatherings, creative activities, or shared interests.
- **For Those in Relationships:** Focus on celebrating your bond with your partner through thoughtful gestures, open communication, and quality time together. The Scorpio energy later in the month deepens intimacy and emotional connection.

**Advice:** Be authentic and confident in your interactions. Use the Libra energy to celebrate love and the Scorpio energy to strengthen trust and commitment.

## *Health*

Health-wise, October encourages Libra to maintain balance and consistency in wellness routines.

- **Strengths:** The Libra energy supports self-care practices that promote physical and mental well-being. Activities like yoga, meditation, or creative hobbies will keep you energized and positive.
- **Challenges:** Stress from social or professional commitments may affect your energy levels if not managed effectively.

**Advice:** Focus on relaxation and prioritize routines that support both your physical and emotional health. Stay hydrated, eat well, and get enough rest to recharge.

## *Be Careful*

- **Overcommitting:** Avoid taking on too many responsibilities, as this could lead to stress or burnout.
- **Indecisiveness:** Don't let your desire to weigh all options prevent you from making important decisions.
- **Neglecting Self-Care:** Balance your busy schedule with moments of relaxation to maintain well-being.

## *Advice*

1. **Shine Bright:** Use Libra energy to express yourself, build connections, and take bold steps toward your goals.
2. **Deepen Emotional Growth:** Embrace Scorpio energy to reflect on your priorities and strengthen meaningful relationships.
3. **Maintain Balance:** Focus on self-care and disciplined planning to sustain energy and clarity throughout the month.
4.

- **Lucky Days:** October 9, 17, and 28 – Ideal for creative projects, decision-making, or celebrating milestones.
- **Lucky Color:** Royal Blue – This color symbolizes confidence, harmony, and success.
- **Affirmation for October:** *"I celebrate my journey and align my actions with my highest potential."*

October 2025 is a month of celebration and transformation for Libra. By focusing on meaningful connections, creative expression, and thoughtful planning, you'll navigate this vibrant period with confidence and clarity.

# November

November 2025 is a month of introspection, transformation, and emotional growth for Libra. With the Sun in Scorpio for most of the month, the focus is on deepening connections, exploring your inner self, and aligning with your long-term goals. As the Sun transitions into Sagittarius later in November, the energy lightens, encouraging optimism, exploration, and a broader perspective on life. This blend of intensity and expansion offers opportunities for meaningful change and growth.

## *Work*

November emphasizes strategic planning and focus in Libra's professional life.

- **Opportunities:** The Scorpio energy supports diving into complex tasks, tackling long-term projects, and refining your strategies. Mid-month is ideal for developing innovative solutions or addressing workplace dynamics. The Sagittarius influence later in the month inspires collaboration, networking, and pursuing exciting career opportunities.
- **Challenges:** Balancing your natural charm with Scorpio's intensity may feel challenging, especially

when handling emotionally charged situations at work.

**Advice:** Use Scorpio's focus to tackle intricate projects and Sagittarius's optimism to explore new opportunities. Maintain professionalism and clarity in your communications.

## *Finance*

Your financial outlook in November emphasizes careful planning and potential gains.

- **Opportunities:** Financial growth may come from investments, bonuses, or partnerships that align with your long-term goals. This is also a good time to focus on savings and reducing unnecessary expenses.
- **Challenges:** Avoid impulsive financial decisions, particularly during moments of emotional intensity or excitement.

**Advice:** Stick to a disciplined budget and seek professional advice if considering significant financial moves.

## Love

November brings depth and transformation to Libra's love life, with Venus enhancing emotional connection and trust.

- **For Singles:** This is a powerful time for meaningful romantic encounters. You may meet someone who resonates with your values and emotional needs, particularly through work, shared activities, or introspective moments.
- **For Those in Relationships:** Focus on deepening trust and resolving past misunderstandings. Open communication and shared experiences will strengthen your bond.

**Advice:** Be authentic and patient in your interactions. Use Scorpio's transformative energy to nurture intimacy and Sagittarius's adventurous energy to reignite passion.

## Health

Health-wise, November encourages Libra to focus on emotional and physical well-being.

- **Strengths:** The Scorpio energy supports detoxifying practices, such as journaling, meditation, or refining your diet.

- **Challenges:** Stress or overthinking may impact your mental clarity and energy levels if not managed effectively.

**Advice:** Incorporate mindfulness practices into your daily routine. Maintain consistency in your wellness habits and prioritize rest to recharge your body and mind.

### *Be Careful*

- **Overthinking:** Avoid dwelling on past mistakes or becoming overly critical of yourself. Focus on progress, not perfection.
- **Neglecting Balance:** Ensure you're devoting time to both introspection and social engagement to avoid feeling isolated.
- **Impulsiveness:** Think carefully before making major financial or personal decisions.

### *Advice*

1. **Focus on Transformation:** Use Scorpio energy to realign with your priorities and embrace meaningful change.
2. **Explore and Expand:** As Sagittarius season begins, shift your focus to optimism, exploration, and building new connections.

3. **Nurture Relationships:** Strengthen bonds with loved ones by being present, supportive, and open to vulnerability.

## *Additional Tips*

- **Lucky Days:** November 8, 16, and 25 – Ideal for introspection, decision-making, or creative pursuits.
- **Lucky Color:** Deep Maroon – This color symbolizes strength, transformation, and emotional depth.
- **Affirmation for November:** *"I embrace transformation and align my actions with my inner truth, creating harmony and growth in my life."*

November 2025 is a month of introspection and renewal for Libra. By focusing on meaningful connections, thoughtful planning, and self-care, you'll navigate this transformative period with confidence and clarity.

# December

December 2025 is a month of reflection, celebration, and forward planning for Libra. With the Sun in Sagittarius for most of the month, the energy emphasizes optimism, exploration, and connecting with others. As the Sun transitions into Capricorn later in December, the focus shifts to grounding, organization, and setting the stage for success in the coming year. This combination of adventurous spirit and practical preparation makes December a time of joy, growth, and strategic planning.

## *Work*

December emphasizes collaboration, innovation, and strategic goal-setting in Libra's professional life.

- **Opportunities:** The Sagittarius energy supports networking, brainstorming, and creative problem-solving. Mid-month is ideal for exploring new career opportunities or solidifying partnerships. The Capricorn influence later in the month encourages practical planning and organizing for long-term success.
- **Challenges:** Balancing your desire for social engagement with the need to focus on work may

feel challenging. Avoid procrastination or overextending yourself.

**Advice:** Use Sagittarius energy to explore opportunities and Capricorn energy to ensure your plans are realistic and actionable.

## *Finance*

Your financial outlook in December highlights balance and preparation for the year ahead.

- **Opportunities:** Financial gains may come from bonuses, year-end rewards, or the results of past efforts. This is a favorable time to revisit your budget and plan for upcoming expenses or investments.
- **Challenges:** Holiday spending may tempt you to overspend on gifts, travel, or social activities.

**Advice:** Stick to your financial goals and prioritize saving for future plans over short-term indulgences.

## *Love*

December brings warmth and connection to Libra's love life, with Venus enhancing harmony and joy in relationships.

- **For Singles:** Social events, travel, or gatherings with friends may lead to exciting romantic opportunities. Look for connections that resonate with your values and intellectual curiosity.
- **For Those in Relationships:** Focus on celebrating your bond with your partner through shared experiences and thoughtful gestures. Late December is ideal for discussing long-term plans or setting new goals together.

**Advice:** Be authentic and open in your interactions. Use the Sagittarius energy to celebrate love and the Capricorn energy to nurture stability in your relationships.

## *Health*

Health-wise, December encourages Libra to balance activity and rest during the festive season.

- **Strengths:** The Sagittarius energy supports physical activity and maintaining a positive mindset. Incorporating fun and engaging activities will help you stay energized.
- **Challenges:** Overindulgence in holiday treats or neglecting self-care routines may affect your well-being if not managed.

**Advice:** Practice moderation and prioritize self-care. Incorporate relaxation techniques and maintain consistency in exercise and nutrition to stay balanced.

## *Be Careful*

- **Overspending:** Avoid exceeding your budget on holiday expenses or spontaneous purchases.
- **Neglecting Rest:** Balance your social commitments with downtime to recharge.
- **Rushed Decisions:** Take your time with year-end planning to ensure your choices align with long-term goals.

## *Advice*

1. **Celebrate and Reflect:** Use Sagittarius energy to connect with loved ones, celebrate your achievements, and reflect on your journey.
2. **Plan for the Future:** Embrace Capricorn energy to set clear, achievable goals for 2026.
3. **Prioritize Self-Care:** Maintain balance by dedicating time to relaxation and meaningful connections.

## *Additional Tips*

- **Lucky Days:** December 10, 18, and 29 – Ideal for reflection, celebration, or decision-making.

- **Lucky Color:** Ruby Red – This color symbolizes passion, grounding, and joy.
- **Affirmation for December:** *"I celebrate my journey and prepare for a future filled with harmony, growth, and purpose."*

December 2025 is a month of celebration and preparation for Libra. By balancing joy with thoughtful planning and self-care, you'll close the year on a high note and set the stage for a fulfilling 2026.

Good Luck
For
2025